CAP

Good Ol' A Cappella

Contemporary
A Cappella Songbook

TTBB Series
Volume 1

A Cappella Arrangements by
Deke Sharon &
Anne Raugh

EXCLUSIVELY DISTRIBUTED BY
HAL•LEONARD®
CORPORATION
7777 W. BLUEMOUND RD. P.O. BOX 13819 MILWAUKEE, WI 53213

Available from Contemporary A Cappella Publishing

The Contemporary A Cappella Songbook Collection:

SATB Series	
Volume 1	HL08741649
Volume 2	HL08741650
Volume 3 – I Feel Good	HL08742598
Volume 4 – Shout!	HL08743512
SSAA Series	
Natural Woman	HL08742904
TTBB Series	
Volume 1 – Good Ol' A Cappella	HL08743513
Volume 2 – Sh-Boom	HL08743514
Love Songs A Cappella	HL08743515
Jazz Standards A Cappella	HL08743235
A CASA Christmas	HL08741651
Songs for All Occasions	HL08742050
Continuum: The First Songbook of Sweet Honey in the Rock	HL08742029
The Collegiate A Cappella Arranging Manual	HL08742599

Available wherever songbooks are sold, or online at *www.a-cappella.com* and *www.casa.org*.

Part-predominant learning tapes are available directly from Mainely A CAPPELLA for the arrangements in:

Contemporary A Cappella Songbook, SATB Series – Volume 1
Contemporary A Cappella Songbook, SATB Series – Volume 2
A CASA Christmas

Call 1.800.827.2936, email *order@a-cappella.com* or order online at *www.a-cappella.com* and specify Soprano, Alto, Tenor, Bass, or a set of all four.

TABLE OF CONTENTS

Cover photo: Ross Mizrahi, Sons of Pitches

Photo: Don Gooding

Good Old Acapella

Arranged by
Deke Sharon and Anne Raugh

Words and Music by
L. Carter and O. Nevada

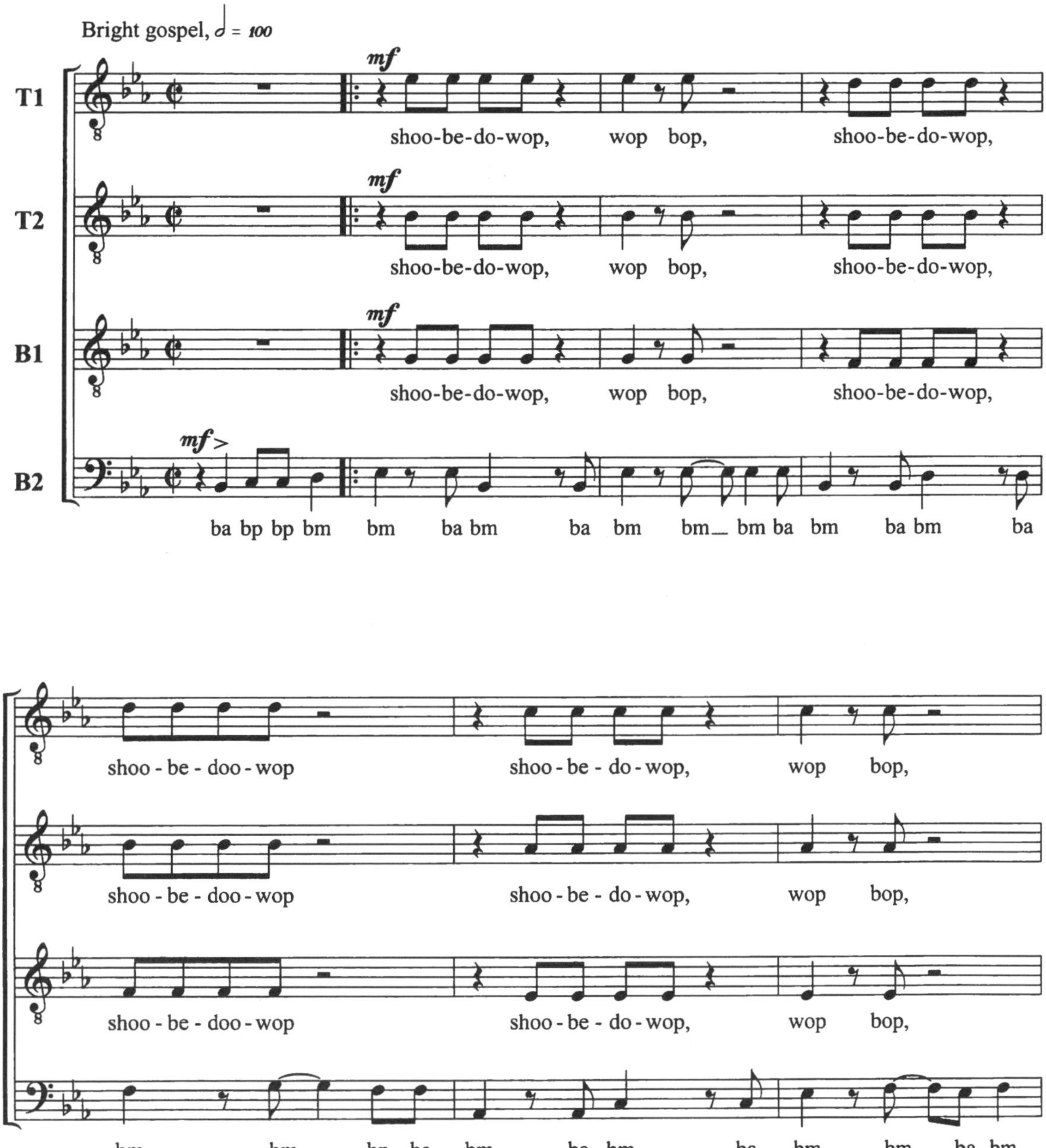

1
2
shoo-be-do-wop, shoo-be-doo-wop hoo hoo hoo
shoo-be-do-wop, shoo-be-doo-wop hoo hoo hoo
shoo-be-do-wop, shoo-be-doo-wop hoo hoo hoo There's a light
shoo-be-do-wop, shoo-be-doo-wop, ba ba ba hoo hoo hoo, ba bo bo bm
12
oo
oo
that's from my win - dow, and it shines down on the street. There's some
bm ba bm ba bm bm bm ba bm ba bm ba bm bm bp ba
oo, good old har - mo - ny.
oo, good old har - mo - ny.
guys stand - ing on the cor - ner, They're mak - ing some good old har - mo - ny.
bm ba bm ba bm bm ba bm good old har - mo - ny.

20
hoo
hoo
Now, this light that's from my win - dow sets the stage for the street cor-ner sym-pho - ny.
ba bp bp bm bm ba bm ba bm bm bm ba bm ba bm ba
oo
good old har-mo - ny.
oo
good old har-mo - ny.
Let it shine, let them sing, and make that good old har-mo - ny.
bm bm bp ba bm ba bm ba bm bm ba bm good old har-mo - ny.
28
soul to soul,
soul to soul,
Sing - ing soul to soul, broth-er to broth - er,
soul to soul,

broth-er to broth - er, a cap-pel - la, sounds good to me.
broth-er to broth - er, a cap-pel - la, sounds good to me.
a cap-pel - la, and it sounds good to me.
broth-er to broth - er, a cap-pel - la, sounds good to me.
37
1
2
hoo
hoo
Sing - ing There's a sound in the neigh-bor - hood, and it's
ba bp bp bm bm ba bm ba bm bm bm ba
oo
oo
sound - ing might - y good. There's some guys stand - ing un - der the light,
bm ba bm ba bm bm bp ba bm ba bm ba

sing - ing a - gain to - night, hoo
sing - ing a - gain to - night, hoo
And they're sing - ing a - gain to - night, Sing - ing that
bm bm ba bm sing - ing a - gain to - night, ba bp bp bm
45
oo
oo
good old a cap-pel - la, That sounds so dog - gone sweet. Let them
bm ba bm ba bm bm bm ba bm ba bm ba bm bm bp ba
good old har - mo - ny,
good old har - mo - ny,
sing, let them dance, and make that good old har - mo - ny, Sing - ing
bm ba bm ba bm bm ba bm good old har - mo - ny,

53
oo, soul to soul, oo, broth - er to broth - er,
oo, soul to soul, oo, broth - er to broth - er,
soul to soul, and broth - er to broth - er,
oo, soul to soul, oo, broth - er to broth - er,
1
oo, a cap - pel - la sounds good to me.
oo, a cap - pel - la sounds good to me.
a cap - pel - la, and it sounds good to me. Sing - ing
oo, a cap - pel - la sounds good to me.
2
62
mp
Be - fore I turn out my light, Say "good - night" to an - oth - er night,
Be - fore I turn out my light, Say "good - night" to an - oth - er night,
Be - fore I turn out my light, Say "good - night" to an - oth - er night,
Be - fore I turn out my light, Say "good - night" to an - oth - er night,

Before I rest my weary head, upon my warm and waiting bed.
70
cresc. poco a poco
I'm going to get on my knees and pray, Tell the Lord to give
me just one more day, "Oh Lord, hear my plea, music
That music

78
mf
means so much to me."
oo, soul to soul,
means so much to me." And I'm sing - ing soul to soul, and
means so much to me." dm bah dm bah soul to soul, bah bah
oo broth - er to broth - er, oo,
broth - er to broth - er, a cap - pel - la,
dm bah dm bah broth - er to broth - er, dm bah dm bah
a cap - pel - la, sounds good to me. hoo hoo
and it sounds good to me. Sing - ing
a cap - pel - la, sounds good to me. bah bah dm bah bah

87
2
shoo - be - do - wop, wop bop, shoo - be - do - wop,
shoo - be - do - wop, wop bop, shoo - be - do - wop,
shoo - be - do - wop, wop bop, shoo - be - do - wop,
ba bp bp bm bm ba bm ba bm bm bm ba bm ba bm ba
shoo - be - doo - wop shoo - be - do - wop, wop bop,
shoo - be - doo - wop shoo - be - do - wop, wop bop,
shoo - be - doo - wop shoo - be - do - wop, wop bop,
bm bm bp ba bm ba bm ba bm bm ba bm
1
2
shoo - be - do - wop, shoo - be - doo - wop oh, oh, yeah!
shoo - be - do - wop, shoo - be - doo - wop oh, oh, yeah!
shoo - be - do - wop, shoo - be - doo - wop oh, oh, yeah!
shoo - be - do - wop, shoo - be - doo - wop, ba ba ba oh, oh, yeah!

Stand By Me

Arranged by
Deke Sharon and Anne Raugh

Words and Music by
Ben E. King, Jerry Leiber and Mike Stoller

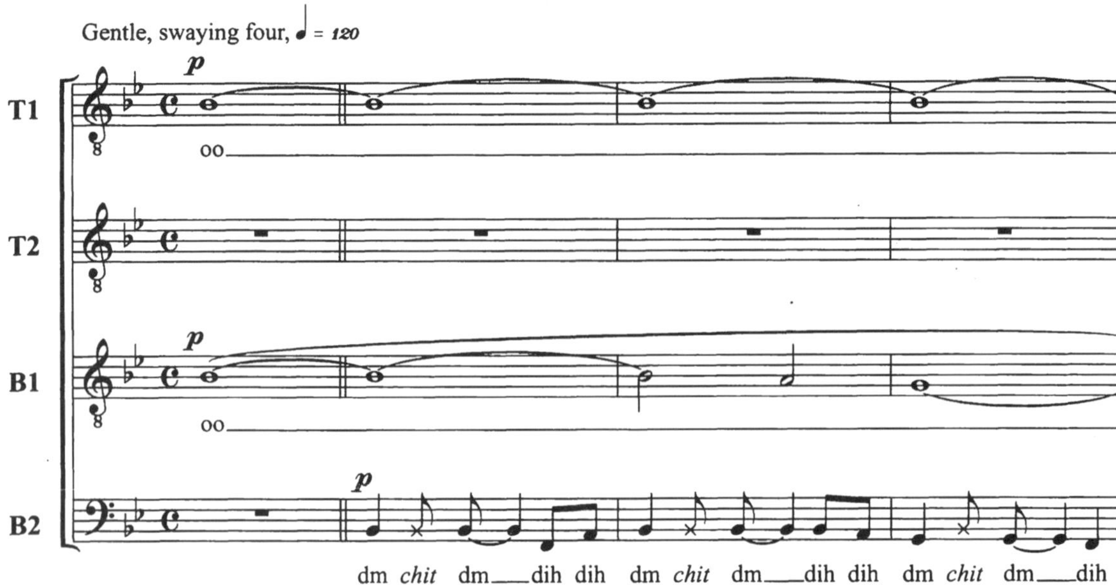

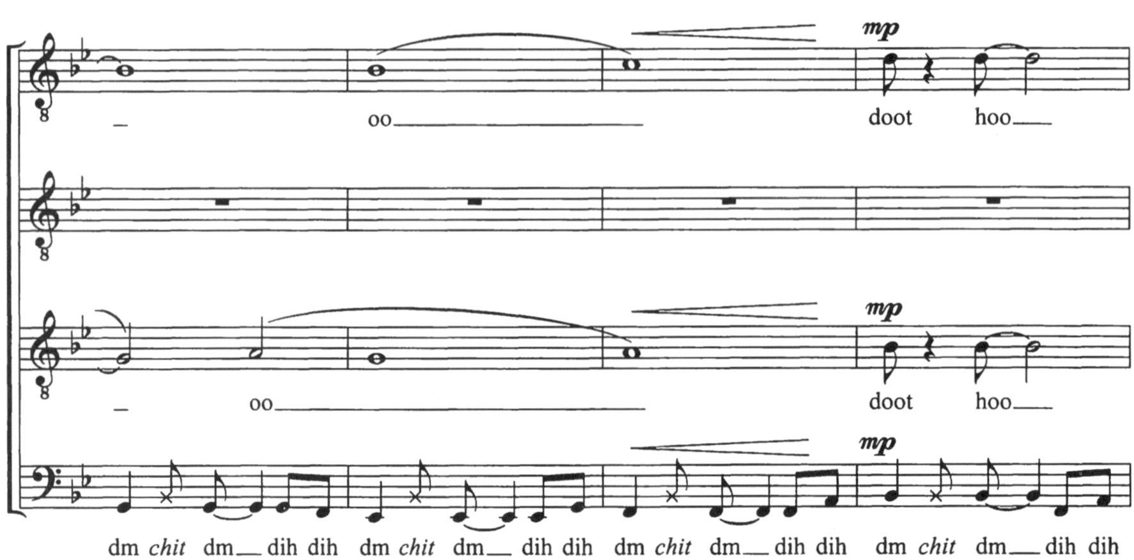

10
doot hoo doot hoo doot hoo
mp
When the night has come
doot hoo doot hoo doot hoo
dm chit dm dih dih dm chit dm dih dih dm chit dm dih dih
doot hoo doot hoo doot hoo
and the land is dark, and the moon is the
doot hoo doot hoo doot hoo
dm chit dm dih dm chit dm dih dih dm chit dm dih dih
doot hoo doot hoo doot hoo
on - ly light we'll see. No I won't
doot hoo doot hoo doot hoo
mf
dm chit dm dih dih dm chit dm dih dih dm chit dm dih dih

18
mf
no I won't, no no I won't be a - fraid, no I won't, no
mf
be a - fraid, No I won't be a-
mf
no I won't, no no I won't be a - fraid, no I won't, no
dm chit dm dih dih dm chit dm dih dih dm chit dm dih
no I won't be a - fraid, just as long as you stand by me.
fraid, Just as long as you stand, stand by
no I won't be a - fraid, just as long as you stand by me.
dm chit dm dih dih dm chit dm dih dih dm chit dm dih dih
26
Dar - lin', Dar - lin' stand by me,
me. Dar - lin', Dar - lin' Dar - lin', stand by me,
Oh, Dar - lin', stand by me,
dm chit dm dih dih dm. Dar - lin', Dar - lin' stand by me,

oh stand by me, oh
Dar-lin', stand by me, Dar-lin', stand by me, Dar-lin', stand by me,
Dar-lin', stand by me, Dar-lin', stand by me, Dar-lin', stand by me,
stand by me, stand by me, stand by me,
To Coda
stand, stand by me, stand by me,
stand me.
stand me.
dm dm dih dih dm dm dih dih dm dm dih dih
34
mp
oo
mp
oo
mp
oo
mp
dm. If the sky that we look up-on should tum-ble and

oo
oo
oo
oo
oo
fall, Or the moun - tains should crum - ble to the sea.
42
no I won't cry no I won't no I won't
I won't cry I won't cry No I
no I won't cry no I won't shed a tear, just as long as you stand
won't shed a tear, Just as long as you stand

D.S. al Coda
by me. Dar - lin', Dar - lin'
by me. Dar - lin', Dar - lin'
by me. Oh,
stand by me. Dar - lin', Dar - lin'
50
dim. and rit. through to end
stand by me, woah, stand,
me, oh stand by me,
me, oh stand by me,
stand by me, Dar - lin' stand by me, dm dih dih
stand by me, stand by me, stand by me,
stand by me.
stand by me.
dm dm dih dih dm dm dih dih dm dm, stand by me.

Good Lovin'

Arranged by
Deke Sharon and Anne Raugh

Words and Music by
Rudy Clark and Arthur Resnick

dih ba dih dit dit dit ba dih ba dit dih ba dih dit dit
now, So I asked my fam' - ly doc -
tight. Said don't ya, don't you want your dad -
dih ba dih dit dit dit ba dih ba dit dih ba dih dit dit
bop ba dih dit dit dit ba dih ba dit bop ba dih dit dit
dit ba dih ba dit dih ba dih dit dit dit ba dih ba dit
tor 'bout what I had now. I said, "Now,
dy to be all right? I said, "Now,
dit ba dih ba dit dih ba dih dit dit dit ba dih ba dit
dit ba dih ba dit bop ba dih dit dit dit ba dih ba dit
13
hoo, doc - tor, hey, doc - tor,
hoo, ba - by, hey, ba - by,
doc - tor, Mis - ter M. D.
ba - by, woah it's for sure.
hoo, doc - tor, hey, doc - tor,
hoo, ba - by, hey, ba - by,
bop ba dih dit dit dit ba dih ba dit bop ba dih dit dit

please, doc - tor,
please, ba - by,
woah, can you tell me what's ail - ing
I got the fe - ver, you got the
please, doc - tor,
please, ba - by,
dit ba dih ba dit bop ba dih dit dit dit ba dih ba dit
21
oh, doc - tor, He said, Yeah,
oh, ba - by, She said, Yeah,
me?" He said, "Yeah, yeah, yeah, yeah, yeah,
cure." She said, "Yeah, yeah, yeah, yeah, yeah,
oh, doc - tor, He said, Yeah,
oh, ba - by, She said, Yeah,
bop ba dih dit dit dit He said, Yeah,
She said, Yeah,
cresc.
yeah, yeah, yeah, yeah, yeah, oo, doc - tor told
yeah, yeah, yeah, yeah, yeah, oo, ba - by knows
All you need,
All you need,
yeah, yeah, yeah, yeah, yeah, oo, doc - tor told
yeah, yeah, yeah, yeah, yeah, oo, ba - by knows
yeah, yeah, yeah, yeah, yeah, oo, doc - tor told
yeah, yeah, yeah, yeah, yeah, oo, ba - by knows

cresc.
me all I real-ly need, yeah, Good
just what I real-ly need, yeah, Good
all you real-ly need,"
all you real-ly need,"
oh yeah! Good
29
lov-in', dih dit dit dit ba dit, good lov-in', dih dit dit
'Cause you got to have love, Ev-'ry-bod-y got
lov - in', dih dit dit dit ba dit, good lov - in', dih dit dit
dit ba dit, good lov-in', dih dit dit dit ba dit, good
to have love, Lit - tle bit of love, Now ba-by good
dit ba dit, good lov - in', dih dit dit dit ba dit, good

35
love, bop ba da dat da dap bap ba
love, bop ba da dat da dap bap ba So, come on ba-
love, bop ba da dat da dap bap ba
love, bop ba da dat da dap bap ba da da da
Good love!
Good love!
Good love!
good good good good good good, Good love!

Up on the Roof

Arranged by
Deke Sharon and Anne Raugh

Words and Music by
Gerry Goffin and Carole King

7
doo dt doo, climb way up to the top of the stairs,
doo dt doo. get a - way from that hust - ling crowd,
doo dt doo, climb way up to the top of the stairs,
doo dt doo. get a - way from that hust - ling crowd,
I climb way up to the top of the stairs, and
I get a - way from that hust - ling crowd, and
doo dt doo, climb way up to the top of the stairs,
doo dt doo. get a - way from that hust - ling crowd,
ah oo, doo doo dt doo doo dt doo
ah oo, doo doo dt doo doo dt doo
ah oo, doo doo dt doo doo dt doo
ah oo, doo doo dt doo doo dt doo
all my cares just drift right in - to space.
all that rat - race noise down in the street.
ah oo, doo doo dt doo doo dt doo
ah oo, doo doo dt doo doo dt doo
13
mf
doo dt doo, On the roof's the on - ly place I
doo dt doo. night the stars put on a show for
doo dt doo, On the roof's the on - ly place I
doo dt doo. night the stars put on a show for
On the roof's the on - ly place I
At night the stars put on a show for
doo dt doo, On the roof's the on - ly place I
doo dt doo. night the stars put on a show for

know, doo dt doo doo doo dt doo, ah
free, doo dt doo doo doo dt doo, ah
know, doo dt doo doo doo dt doo, ah
free, doo dt doo doo doo dt doo, ah
know Where you just have to wish to make it so.
free, And Dar-ling you can share it all with me.
know, doo dt doo doo doo dt doo, ah
free, doo dt doo doo doo dt doo, ah
1
2
oh, oo
oh,
oh, Up on the roof,
oh,
Up on the roof. When I keep tell-ing you that
oh, Up on the roof,
oh,
24
Follow lead
right smack mid-dle of town, found a par-a-dise
right smack mid-dle of town, found a par-a-dise
ad lib.
right smack dab in the mid-dle of town, I found a par-a-dise
right smack mid-dle of town, found a par-a-dise

a tempo
doo doo dt doo doo dt doo doo dt doo.
doo doo dt doo doo dt doo doo dt doo.
that's trou-ble proof. And if
doo doo dt doo doo dt doo doo dt doo.
30
this old world starts get - ting you down, oo,
this old world starts get - ting you down, oo,
this old world starts get - ting you down, there's room e - nough for two
this old world starts get - ting you down, oo,
doo dt doo doo dt doo doo,
doo dt doo doo dt doo doo,
up on the roof, up on the roof,
doo dt doo doo dt doo doo,

35
Come on, come on, come on, come on, com on, come on! Come on babe,
Come on, come on, come on, come on, com on, come on! Come on babe,
Come on babe,
Come on, come on, come on, come on, com on, come on! Come on babe,
come on babe, up on the roof.
come on babe, up on the roof.
come on babe, up on the roof.
come on babe, up on the roof.
Repeat ad lib.
Last time
Come on babe, Up on the roof.
Come on babe, Up on the roof.
Come on babe, Up on the roof.
Up on the roof, babe, Up on the roof.

Goodnight, Sweetheart, Goodnight

(Goodnight, It's Time to Go)

Arranged by
Deke Sharon and Anne Raugh

Words and Music by
James Hudson and Calvin Carter

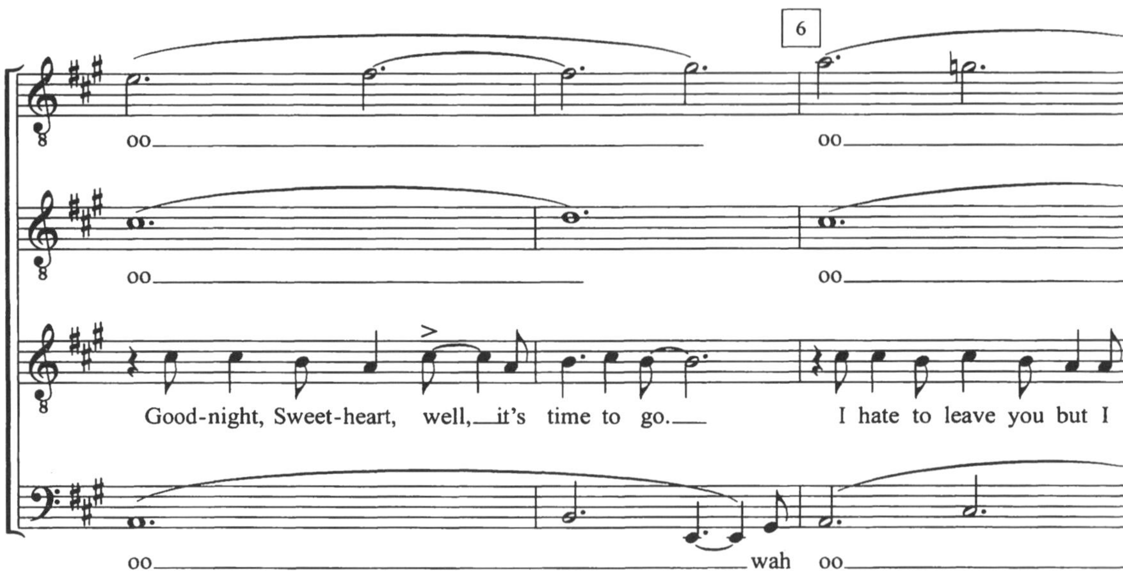

oo
oo
real-ly must say, Good-night, Sweet-heart, good-night.
Good-night, Sweet-heart, good, dit di-dit dit di-dit dit di-dit dit
10
mf
Good-night, Sweet-heart, well, it's time to go.
Melody
mf
Good-night, Sweet-heart, well, it's time to go.
mf
Good-night, Sweet-heart, well, it's time to go.
mf
bom ba dm, ba dm bm dit di-dit dit
Good-night, Sweet-heart, well, it's time to go. whoa,
Good-night, Sweet-heart, well, it's time to go.
Good-night, Sweet-heart, well, it's time to go.
bom ba-dm ba dm bm ba da da da da

I hate to leave you but I real-ly must say, Good-night, Sweet - heart, good - night.
I hate to leave you but I real-ly must say, Good-night, Sweet - heart, good - night.
I hate to leave you but I real-ly must say, Good-night, Sweet - heart, good - night.
dm dm ba dm dm ba dm dm ba dm dm, Good-night, Sweet - heart, good - night,
18
Well, doot doot doot doot doot doot doot doot
doot doot doot doot doot doot doot doot
Well, doot doot doot doot doot doot doot doot
doot doot doot doot doot doot doot doot
Well, doot doot doot doot doot doot doot doot
doot doot doot doot doot doot doot doot
Good-night, Well, it's three o' - clock in the morn - ing.
moth-er and your fa - ther,
doot doot doot doot just can't treat you, doot doot doot doot
doot doot doot doot if I stay too, doot doot doot doot
doot doot doot doot just can't treat you, doot doot doot doot
doot doot doot doot if I stay too, doot doot doot doot
doot doot doot doot just can't treat you, doot doot doot doot
doot doot doot doot if I stay too, doot doot doot doot
Ba - by, I just can't treat you right. Well, I hate to leave you, ba - by, I
Might hear if I stay here too long. One kiss and we'll part, And

don't mean may - be, be-cause I love you
you'll be go - ing, I hate to see you
don't mean may - be, be-cause I love you
you'll be go - ing, I hate to see you
don't mean may - be, be - cause I love you
you'll be go - ing, you know I hate to see you
don't mean may - be, oo
you'll be go - ing, oo
26
so.
go.
Good-night, Sweet-heart, well, it's
dit di-dit dit di-dit dit di-dit dit
bom ba dm, ba
time to go.
Good-night, Sweet-heart, well, it's
dm bm dit di-dit dit
bom ba - dm ba

time to go. whoa, I hate to leave you but I
time to go. I hate to leave you but I
time to go. I hate to leave you but I
dm bm ba da da da da dm dm ba dm dm ba
real - ly must say, Good - night, Sweet - heart, good - night.
real - ly must say, Good - night, Sweet - heart, good - night.
real - ly must say, Good - night, Sweet - heart, good - night.
dm dm ba dm dm, Good - night, Sweet - heart, good - night,
1
2
Good - night. Now, Good - night.
Good - night. Now, Good - night.
Good - night. Now, Good - night.
Good - night. Now, your Good - night.

PERFORMANCE NOTES

When it comes to popular music, traditional Western music notation is, well, inadequate. Use your knowledge of the original songs and internal sense of pop music to turn the black dots on the page into loose, rhythmic rock and roll. This is especially true with solo lines: use the notated solos only as a rough guide (were we to notate the solos exactly as in the originals, they'd often be wildly complex).

Every group is different, and no arrangement can suit them all perfectly, so we encourage you to change our arrangements in any way to better suit your own ensemble.

Good Old Acapella: Beware of rushing the frequent anticipations; have your singers snap or clap if you're losing time. The verse at measure 62 will sound all the more impressive if your singers' phrasing, breathing and articulation are very tight.

Stand By Me: The *chit* in the bass line should be without pitch or tone – almost *cht*. All of the solo lines should be very loose and the backgrounds light.

Good Lovin': Set an initial brisk tempo, but be careful not to let the syncopations pull the tempo up. If you have an extra voice you can spare, vocal percussion would work well. Tight background figures that are energetic without being loud will help keep the excitement level high throughout.

Up On The Roof: Make sure to hold all the notes their full value to preclude too much open space between harmonic passages. If you'd like to sing this arrangement in the same key as the Nylons (the version upon which this one is based) take the entire arrangement up a whole step to B-flat.

Goodnight, Sweetheart, Goodnight: An excellent closer or encore – don't hesitate to get the audience to sing along. Be particularly careful with the background figures under the bass solo: a light touch here will let the bass enjoy a rare melodic line.

WHAT IS CASA?

The Contemporary A Cappella Society

is a non-profit organization formed in 1990 to foster and promote a cappella music. We serve both the fan and the performer.

Membership Levels

BASIC: For only $35 a year ($25 with student ID; $40 outside the U.S.), basic membership includes a subscription to the Contemporary A Cappella News (CAN). The CAN is a bi-monthly newsletter that includes international news and concert calendars, guest columns by big names in the a cappella industry, interviews with top groups, how-to articles and album reviews.

PREMIUM: For those in a group or serious about a cappella, premium membership at $50 a year ($35 with student ID; $55 outside the U.S.) includes the benefits of basic membership plus: one free classified ad in the CAN; the A Cappella Directory; discounts on custom arrangements from the Ultimate A Cappella Arranging Service; discounts on recordings and songbooks from Mainely A Cappella; and discounts on other a cappella-related merchandise and services, including album production. As an added benefit, if one member of a group joins at the Premium level, other members of the group may receive additional copies of the CAN for just $10 a year (each).

SPONSOR: For $100 a year ($110 outside the U.S.), Sponsors enjoy all the benefits of premium membership plus a custom-pressed CD copy of each A Cappella Radio International (ARI) monthly broadcast, and one complementary copy of a CASA publication (such as *Starting an A Cappella Group*).

BENEFACTOR: For $250 a year, Benefactors enjoy all the benefits of Sponsors plus: one hot-off-the-press copy of the annual *Best of College A Cappella (BOCA)* CD; the annual *Contemporary A Cappella Recording Awards (CARA)* CD; and one complementary copy of any CASA-produced CD.

PATRON: For $500 a year, Patrons enjoy all of the above plus special VIP benefits throughout the year, including access to private, CASA-sponsored concerts.

CASA Productions

- The **Urban Harmony Movement**, a free community enhancing singing programs for teens and adults
- The **A Cappella Summit**, which brings hundreds of fans, performers and enthusiasts together for two days of seminars, concerts and workshops
- The **Contemporary A Cappella Recording Awards**, a yearly quest for the best recorded a cappella music from around the globe
- **A Cappella Community Awards**, allowing fans to vote for their favorite groups
- The **A Cappella Summit**, which brings hundreds of fans, performers and enthusiasts together for two days of seminars, concerts and workshops
- The **Northern Harmony** Canadian a cappella festival and competition
- The **International Championship of Collegiate A Cappella**, a competition involving college groups of all styles from across North America
- The **A Cappella Almanac**, the complete a cappella website with links to all CASA programs and everything else you might want to know about a cappella
- The **International A Cappella Recording Archives**, a library of over 3,000 a cappella recordings

- **A Cappella Radio International**, a monthly program of news and interviews, broadcast internationally and on the World Wide Web
- **Contemporary A Cappella Recording Awards CD**, including the best submissions from nominees and winners
- The **Urban Harmony Movement R&B CD**, featuring professional and collegiate groups
- The **Northern Harmony CD**, featuring performances from the inaugural year of that festival
- The **Best of College A Cappella (BOCA) CD** series, produced jointly with Mainely A Cappella
- **Class Notes: The Best of Highschool A Cappella CD**, a compilation of outstanding highschool groups
- The **Definitive A Cappella Press Kit**, a guide for groups putting together their own promotional material
- **Producing the Ultimate A Cappella Show**, a how-to manual covering everything from single-group concerts to festivals
- **Starting an A Cappella Group**, a basic guide to starting up your own group for fun or profit

TO JOIN, send a check to:

CASA
PMB 1449
1850 Union Street #4
San Francisco, CA 94123
USA

For more information, drop us a line:

Phone: 1.415.563.5224
Fax: 1.415.921.2834
Email: casa@casa.org
World Wide Web: http://www.casa.org/

Other A Cappella Resources

MAINELY A CAPPELLA (MAC)
MAC is a mail-order catalog published annually with quarterly updates. It features more than 2,000 titles, including rare and international releases. The catalog represents a wide range of styles and genres - from the latest in pop, jazz and world bands to classical ensembles and barbershop harmonies.

MAC Yak
Mainely A CAPPELLA'S electronic newsletter features new releases, pre-releases, and is the only place to find great sale items.

VARSITY VOCALS
Varsity Vocals is a student a cappella outreach organization that sponsors five great programs:

The *Best of College A Cappella (BOCA)* annual compilation CD encourages college groups to compete for a place on this sought-after CD.

The *International Championship of Collegiate A Cappella (ICCA)* brings together hundreds of college a cappella singers who compete in regional concerts across North America for a place in the national finals, held in the Avery Fisher Hall of Lincoln Center, New York City.

The *Best of High School A Cappella (BOHSA)* compilation CD features high school groups from all over the world.

Worldwide A Cappella Music Month (WAMM) supports the Music Educator's National Conference *Music in Our Schools Month* during March.

The *Vocal Challenge (VC)* brings the musical expertise of professional a cappella groups to students, to inspire them to achieve higher musical goals.

For more details see: *www.varsityvocals.com*

ON-LINE COMMUNITY
The Mainely A CAPPELLA catalog has a popular home page on the World Wide Web, at *www.a–cappella.com*. There are more than 20,000 RealAudio® and MP3 sound clips to hear, an extensive and continually updated concert calendar, and secure on-line buying. There is also a very active newsgroup on the Internet designed exclusively for a cappella fans: *rec.music.a–cappella* (on the web at *groups.google.com*).

For more information contact us:

PO Box 159
Southwest Harbor, ME 04679
Phone: 1.800.827.2936
International: 1.207.244.7603
Fax: 1.207.244.7613
Email: catalog@a-cappella.com
World Wide Web: www.a-cappella.com
For a FREE catalog call: 1.800.827.2936